ALL THE HONEY

Books by
Rosemerry Wahtola Trommer

Hush: Poems (Middle Creek Publishing, 2020)

Naked for Tea (Able Muse, 2018)

Even Now (Lithic Press, 2016)

The Less I Hold (Turkey Buzzard Press, 2012)

The Miracle Already Happening: Everyday Life with Rumi
    (Liquid Light Press, 2011)

Intimate Landscape: The Four Corners in Poetry & Photography
    (Durango Herald Small Press, 2009)

Holding Three Things at Once (Turkey Buzzard Press, 2008)

More Christmas Angels (Red Rock Press, 2006)

The Christmas Candle Book with Poems of Light
    (Red Rock Press, 2004)

Insatiable: Poems (Sisu Press, 2004)

If You Listen: Poems & Photographs of the San Juan Mountains
    (Western Reflections Press, 2000)

Lunaria: Poems (Sisu Press, 1999)

ALL THE HONEY

—— *Poems* ——

ROSEMERRY WAHTOLA TROMMER

Samara Press
2023

ISBN: 978-1-955140-02-7
Library of Congress Control Number: 2022945302
Printed in the United States of America

Samara Press
www.samarapress.net

Cover painting by Odilon Redon
Designed by Robert E. Blesse

For Eric, Shawnee, and Vivian

CONTENTS

IV. Unfolding into the Moment

A BIT OF A PRELUDE

I wasn't sure I could do it.

When Elizabeth Dilly and Steven Nightingale of Samara Press invited me to create a book that included sensual, playful poems and poems of deep grief, it sounded impossible. How could a poem about Dolly Parton in high heel shoes live in the same book as a poem about the day after my son died?

When we first spoke about a collection, it had been six months since Finn took his life and three months since my father died of kidney failure. My family was reeling with loss. Before the deaths, most of my poems had been about falling in love with the world as it is. After the deaths, I was still writing poems steeped in love, but most were focused on meeting Finn's death—one of my paths toward healing. The tenor of the "after" poems was so different, I couldn't imagine combining the two.

Several weeks after our first conversation, a vision came to me in which Dad and Finn carved the words ALL THE HONEY into my bedroom wall. I think of myself as more practical, less mystical, but I can't pretend the vision didn't happen, nor do I want to. Immediately, I knew I'd been given the title for the book.

That day I considered the phrase as my husband and I skied through the trees on Lizard Head Pass. I came to understand the message this way: Every drop of honey that's ever been made requires two things: 1) nectar to deposit into the honeycomb and 2) pollen to feed the worker bees. One is delectable, and the other, to my taste, vile.

> from sweet nectar
> and bitter pollen
> all the honey

What had at first felt impossible now felt imperative. I wanted to include a broad spectrum of experience and emotion in one book—humor and horror, elation and devastation, love and loss. What's more, I wanted to integrate the different themes throughout the book just as I was being asked to integrate the all-of-it-all-at-once in my own life. It felt thrilling. Healing. Natural. Enlivening.

One of my poetry heroes, Jack Mueller, used to growl at me, and anyone who'd listen, "Power to the paradox." I've never trusted him more.

Rosemerry Wahtola Trommer
Placerville, Colorado
August 29, 2022

I. A Deeper Listening

me the vase
with a thousand thin fractures
you the slightest touch

&

deep desert canyon of the heart—
it remembers when
it was ocean

&

reclaiming them
as a place for rest—
these thousand-petalled thoughts

THE BAILIFF OF THE HEART

The Bailiff of the Heart wears comfortable shoes—
she knows she'll be standing
outside the heart's door

for a long, long time,
while inside the chamber
the many voices of love deliberate.

It's never so simple as innocent or guilty.
The heart is full of what ifs and if onlys
and the jury's aware of what's at stake—

nothing less than everything.
The bailiff doesn't mind.
She can hear them in there bellowing,

pleading, reasoning, stonewalling.
She gets them water.
She tells the court to wait.

It's her job to protect their conversation.
She long ago gave up believing in justice.
Still, she believes in love.

MORNING AFTER

Again the chance to praise
the same room, the same floor,
the same view, the same tea,

the same image in the same mirror,
which today is startlingly not the same.
Again the chance to find the miracle

in the leaves that fall, the miracle
in the morning sun, the miracle
in the willows beside the pond.

Again, the chance to fall in love
with the same sky, the same field,
the same dirt, the same broken world.

Again, the chance to show up
with these same tired arms
and put them to work,

the same work as yesterday,
which is to learn to lift up,
to heal, to carry, to build,

to be in the world, to praise
the same room, the same floor,
the same view, the same tea.

WATCHING MY FRIEND PRETEND HER HEART ISN'T BREAKING

On Earth, just a teaspoon of neutron star
would weigh six billion tons. Six billion tons
is equivalent to the weight of every animal
on earth, including insects. Times three.

Six billion tons sounds impossible
until I consider how it is to swallow grief—
just one teaspoon and one may as well have consumed
a neutron star. How dense it is,
how it carries inside it the memory of collapse.
How difficult it is to move then.
How impossible to believe anything
could ever lift that weight.

There are many reasons to treat each other
with great tenderness. One is
the sheer miracle we are here together
on a planet surrounded by dying stars.
One is we cannot see
what anyone else has swallowed.

TEMPLE

O body, cracked bell
that still sings when struck,
O leaky cup,
O broken stem,
I love you, body,
your crooked path,
your crumbling walls,
your faulty math.
I love the way
you stopped believing
you could ever
hold it all,
how you began
to let yourself
become the one
that's being held.
I love the graffiti
on your inner halls—
scrawled names of all
who shaped you.
O body, my wreck,
my holey glove,
my street worn sole,
my crumpled page,
forgive me for years
of trying to fix you,
for believing the fable
of whole,
you, my perfect
wounded heart,
my stuttered hymn,
my sacred
begging bowl.

EMERGING SELF-PORTRAIT

I know now myself as helpless—
helpless the way a rake is helpless,
helpless as knife, as needle,
as match, as pen is helpless.
I know what it is to not function,
despite potential, despite history.
I know how it is to lose all agency,
though once I could stitch,
could fix, could bring light.

I know can't.
I know out of the question,
infeasible, undone, no-go.
Unable to speak. Unable to rise.
This was the moment when love arrived,
love with its ten thousand hands,
love with its perfect skeleton key
to enter every door of me.

Not that I asked.
Not that I deserved it.
Not that I said yes.
But love arrived on grief's strong wings,
and I, a sapped and broken thing,
am learning to know myself as free
when I depend on love's skillful hand,
am learning to trust love,
even when it turns my eyes toward
what I most wish not to see
and love whispers to me,
Is it not beautiful?

What I need tonight is a chair—
the big upholstered kind
that sighs when I sit into it,
the kind that holds me the way
I used to imagine a cloud would hold me—
downy, cozy, comfy, secure
and filled with light.

I need a chair that will make me
not want to get up to do
whatever important thing
I think I must do.
Why do I always think I need
to do something? Why
is it so hard to just sit?

So, I guess, what I really need is a chair
and a seatbelt, the kind
they have on helicopters
with five straps that meet
in the center—though
I think those are self-release,
and we all know I will soon
feel driven to rise and rush,
no matter how cumulonimbus-ish
that chair might feel, no matter
how insistent the straps.

So tonight, what I really need
is a soft chair and a five-strap seat belt
and a giant weighted blanket—
not heavy enough to crush me,
but one with enough gravity

that being still feels like the only real choice.
And if I am still, very still,
and not accomplishing anything for a while,
then perhaps I will meet this grief
I am escaping—not that I am trying
to escape it on purpose,
it's just there is so much important
stuff to do and, perhaps,
let's say I've noticed when I just sit,
just sit,
with nothing to read and nothing to do,
the grief sits with me
and asks nothing of me except
that I meet it.

In that moment,
I remember turning toward grief
is what I most want to do.
In that moment, there is nothing
on any to-do list that could deter me
from meeting this grief.

Oh world, I remember.
I remember right now,
so please, what I need most tonight,
it doesn't matter how soft,
how threadbare,
is a chair.

THE INVITATION

Two nights after he died,
all night I heard the same
one-line story on repeat:
*I am the woman whose son
took his life.* The words
felt full of self-pity,
filled me with hopelessness, doom.
And then a voice came,
a woman's voice, just before dawn,
and it gave me a new shade of truth:
*I am the woman who learns
how to love him now that he's gone.*
It did not change the facts,
but it changed everything
about how I met the facts.
Over a hundred days later,
I am still learning what it means
to love him—how love is
an ocean, a wildfire, a crumb;
how commitment to love changes me,
changes everyone,
invites us to bring our best.
Love is wine, is trampoline,
is an infinite song with a chorus
in which I am sung.
*I am the woman who learns
how to love him now that he's gone.*
May I always be learning how to love—
like a cave. Like a rough-legged hawk.
Like a sun.

HOPE

Hope has holes
in its pockets.
It leaves little
crumb trails
so that we,
when anxious,
can follow it.
Hope's secret:
it doesn't know
the destination—
it knows only
that all roads
begin with one
foot in front
of the other.

LOSING IT

It was a tiny percentage, I knew, but still
there was some French royalty somewhere
in my blood. I would spend hours imagining
myself in my proper place: in a long pink dress

and thin gold crown in a castle on a green hillside,
doing needlepoint, no doubt, and nibbling bon bons,
and so when I again asked my mother
to tell me about that part of our heritage, she told me,

It's so little blood, and you've had so many
skinned knees, I'm pretty sure you've
bled it all out by now. And I was instantly
less grandiose. That was, perhaps, the first identity

I was aware of losing. But soon after
I was no longer blonde. And soon after that,
I no longer lived in Wisconsin. And soon after that,
I was no longer a Scout. Everything I thought

I knew about myself didn't last. Ah,
the litany of losses. Those notions of who we are,
how they shed, they spill, they slip off.
As they're lost, we usually rush to replace them.

I became worker. Lover. Parent. Friend.
We wear them so close, these identities,
that we no longer see them as separate.
We think they're who we are.

What if we skinned not just our knees,
but our thoughts, and let those roles escape?
Who would be left to walk through the field this evening
to see the double rainbow stretched across the east?

CRICKETS

When they sing
it is a kind of love,
a pure-toned,
full-bodied ringing
born of friction.
You could say
it's just a wing stroke
that makes a pulse of sound
that joins with all
the other pulses
to form a river of music,
and you would be right.
But there are many ways
to face the dark.
One is to hide.
One is to prowl.
One is to bring
the bright music
of your body
and offer it
to the night.

REVIVAL

> The day your son died, the person you were died, too.
> —Mirabai Starr

Death came to her
as a blue sky day,
as a feral scream,
as an ambulance
with no need
for its siren.
Death came to her
saying, *Ma'am,*
you don't want
to see your son
this way. Death
knew what it
was doing when
it erased everything
she'd thought she knew
about how to meet a day,
when it scraped her
of who she had been
and left her half barren.
It was habit
that made her
brush her teeth,
routine that helped
her drive the car.
But it was life itself
that inspirited
her, slipping
like starlight
into her every
dark cell, life itself
that whispered

to her death-bent heart,
You are not done
yet with your
loving.

I Want to Listen to Your Absence

I want to listen to your absence
the way I listen to the night—
the way the dark somehow
invites a deeper listening.
I want to hear, for instance,
the way silence fills in
where your voice has been,
or the way the room seems to know itself
by the sound of missing footsteps,
and in this way, I find you
where I cannot find you.
I am thinking of how the night opens up
between the calls of the owl
and how I listen in that interval
not only with my ears, but with my skin.
I want to listen for you with my lungs—
as if every breath is attentive
to the syllables of grief, of love.
I want my heart to angle in
to hear what the silence has to say.
I don't want to hear what I most want to hear—
I want to hear what is really here.
I want to listen and learn from the listening.
I want to listen into your absence
and lean into it the way I lean into the night—
something so much larger than me,
something familiar and always new,
something so present, yet unable to be touched.
I want to hear what is true.

On a Clear Day

The way the field holds
    the shadow of the cottonwood,
        this is how life holds me.

Holds me, no matter my shape.
    Holds me with no effort.
        Holds my darkness and knows it

as weightless, as transient,
    as something that will shift,
        disappear, return, and shift again.

It never says no to me.
    I am still learning to trust life, to trust
        no matter how I show up, I will be held.

Trust that my life is not a problem.
    Trust that as much as I am the shadow,
        I am also the field.

From What I've Tasted of Desire

If without warning the world were to end
at 6:05 tonight, I would like to be holding your hand
at 6:02 and sitting on the back porch
in the low-angled gold August light.
Maybe we would be talking about the birds—
what kind of swallows do you think those are?
And you would say, violet green swallows,
and even if we were not sure it was correct,
it would give us pleasure to know an answer.

We would lean back and watch as they keel
through the air just above our heads.
And at 6:04, we would not know to be concerned
about what would happen next. It is sometimes
better that way, not knowing, I mean,
especially when the cosmos in the garden
are just now in an uprising of bright pink bloom
and the grass in the field is taller
than our legs and if we breathe in
deeply, we can smell the rain is about to come.

OFF THE CLOCK

I want to wake with no sense of what a minute is—
no watch on my hand, no dial on the wall,
no method to measure this life into units of when.
I want to lean into the spell of sunlight like orchids on the sill.
I want to be a question only the moment can answer,
want bergamot to tell me it's time for tea.
And if there is a pressing yes, then let it find me.
Let me feel into the field of my upper back—
how spacious it becomes when I act with integrity.
Let me be rhythm of shadow and birdsong,
let me be rising wind. Let me be time itself,
not the arrow of time, but the infinite sea
and the sand that slips and the silence that swells
in the absence of tick tick tick. I want to wake
to no hands but yours and mine. To be born into the day.
No was. No will. No once. No when.
No deadline. No finish line. No wrong date. No too late.
No too late. Not even a little too late. It would never be too late.

HOW THE HEALING COMES

Healing comes less like a falcon
    with mighty wings,
        and more like an earthworm
    that slowly, slowly moves
beneath it all, tightening up,
    then stretching out, tightening up
        and stretching out, a simple
    two-part rhythm. Some days,
that is all the body can do.
    Contract. Expand. Contract. Expand.
        In the meantime, through this
    artless act, what is dense
becomes porous.
    In the meantime, what is stuck
        and clotted gets moved around.
    What is dead passes through,
is processed by the grit inside.
    There are tunnels now in the soil of me,
        thin channels of recovery—
    a blessed loosening,
a gradual renewal. It's unhurried, but
    I feel it, the air, the rain,
        the life coming in.

The Awakening

When we wake, all people are rivers—
though some are torrents and some mere
trickles, though some break down
obstacles and some slowly meander. We
move from our beds through the banks
of the world, our lives following the course
of the day. Our streams merge with the streams
of others. We are, every day, more each other
and still somehow ourselves. If only we could trust
our uniting currents as unthinkingly as the rivers
follow gravity—always with the least amount
of resistance. How long will we pretend
we are separate?
How long before we find ourselves
joined in the communion of the sea?
All our waters one water.
Every waking an invitation.

SEEKING PURPOSE

> The golden opportunity you are seeking is in yourself. It is
> not in your environment; it is not in luck or chance, or the
> help of others; it is in yourself alone.
> —Orison Swett Marden, *He Can Who Thinks*
> *He Can, and Other Papers on Success in Life*

There were no letters tucked in the trees today,
no handwritten notes tied with red string.
No epistles, no missives, no communiqués.

Some days, a woman wishes the world
would be more direct, more intimate, would just tell her
her purpose, would spell it out in a language she knows.

Include sketches, clear directives. Write her name
on the envelopes so there can be no mistake.
Leave the letters in a place she will find them.

But no. Today, the only message in the trees
is snow. She tries to make meaning of it.
Laughs at the impulse. Reminds herself, Snow is snow.

Isn't it like her to look for meaning?
Next thing you know, she'll be looking
for a message in the clouds. In rivers. In poems. In books.

ALLIUM

While I did not fix
the thing I most
wish to fix, and I
did not do
the most important
thing on my list,
and I did not save
anyone, and I did
not solve the world's
problems, I did
plant the onion sets
in the garden,
pressed my fingers
into the dry earth,
knew myself as
a thin dry start.
Oh patience, good
self. This slow
and quiet growing,
this, too, is
what you are
here to do.

The Dust Speaks

I always come back.
Not out of spite. Not
to annoy you. I settle
here in your home
because I am you.
I am your sloughed off skin.
I'm your hair. I'm your cells.
I'm fibers from your clothes
mixed with bits of dead bugs
and soil and pollen and plastic.
I am the memory
of everywhere you've been
and I am the memory
of what you do
and I come from places
you'll never go.
I can shine, too—
sometimes when the light is right
you see me glitter in the room
and curse me.
But child of the cosmos,
I am here to help you remember
where you came from.
And child of earth,
I am here to help you see
you are one with everything.
I am here to remind you
where you go from here.

Filling My Purse with Commas

All afternoon, each time
I think I should hurry,
I pull out a comma,

such humble punctuation,
and I invite it into the moment,
and the comma does

what it always does, which
is to invite a pause, a small pause,
of course, but a pause long enough

to breathe, to notice what else
is happening, a slight
suggestion that right here

is a perfect place to rest,
yes, how funny I never noticed
before that the comma itself

looks as if it's bowing, nodding
its small dark head to what is,
encouraging us to find

a brief silence and then,
thus refreshed, go on.

SAFETY NET

This morning I woke
  thinking of all the people I love
  and all the people they love
and how big the net of lovers.
  It felt so clear,
   all those invisible ties
interwoven like silken threads
  strong enough to make a mesh
  that for thousands of years
has been woven and rewoven
  to catch us all.
   Sometimes we go on
as if we forget about it.
  Believing only in the fall.
   But the net is just as real.
Every day, with every small kindness,
  with every generous act,
  we strengthen it.
Notice, even now,
  how as the whole world
  seems to be falling,
the net is there for us
  as we walk the day's tightrope.
   Notice how every tie matters.

With the Stars All Around

I wish you the peace of sleep,
your breath a canoe
that carries you
toward the next moment
without any need
for you to touch the oars.
How easily you arrive.

Oh, to trust the world like that—
trust you will be carried,
not just in sleep,
but in waking dreams,
trust no matter how high the waves,
the skiff of grace
has a seat for you.

Oh, to let go of the oars—
there is no steering
toward what comes next.

II. Is This the Path of Love?

desperate for shade
I plant a sapling—
bring it water

&

both hands plunge
into the love poem—
now they're handcuffed there

&

but what if I can't do enough
I said, and love said,
what if you don't try?

THE QUESTION

for Jude Jordan Kalush, who asked the question

All day, I replay these words:
Is this the path of love?
I think of them as I rise,
as I wake my children,
as I wash dishes,
as I drive too close
behind the slow blue Subaru,
Is this the path of love?
Think of these words as I stand in line
at the grocery store,
think of them as I sit on the couch
with my daughter.
Amazing how quickly six words
become compass, the new lens
through which to see myself in the world.
I notice what the question is not.
Not, "Is this right?"
Not, "Is this wrong?"
It just longs to know
how the action of existence
links us to the path of love.
And is it this? Is it this?
All day, I let myself be led by the question.
All day I let myself not be too certain
of the answer. *Is it this?*
Is this the path of love? I ask
as I wait for the next word to come.

MEETING YOUR DEATH

Because there are no clear instructions,
I follow what rises up in me to do.
I fall deeper into love with you.
I look at old pictures.
I don't look at old pictures.
I talk about you. I say nothing.
I walk. I sit. I lie in the grass
and let the earth hold me.
I lie on the sidewalk, dissolve
into sky. I cry. I don't cry.
I ask the world to help me stay open.
I ask again, *Please, let me feel it all.*
I fall deeper in love with the people
still living. I fall deeper in love
with the world that is left—
this world with its spring
and its war and its mornings,
this world with its fruits
that ripen and rot and reseed,
this world that insists
we keep our eyes wide,
this world that opens
when our eyes are closed.
Because there are no clear instructions,
I learn to turn toward the love that is here,
though sometimes what is here is what's not.
There are infinite ways to do this right.
That is the only way.

MORE LOVE, MORE LOVE

> Sorrow is how we learn to love.
> —Rita Mae Brown, *Riding Shotgun*

If sorrow is how we learn to love,
then let us learn.
Already enough sorrow's been sown
for whole continents to erupt
into astonishing tenderness.
Let us learn. Let compassion grow rampant,
like sunflowers along the highway.
Let each act of kindness replant itself
into acres and acres of widespread devotion.
Let us choose love as if our lives depend on it.
The sorrow is great. Let us learn to love greater—
riotous love, expansive love,
love so rooted, so common
we almost forget
the world could look any other way.

Making Breakfast with Dolly

Tonight I read
how Dolly Parton
always wears
high heel shoes
in her kitchen.
Don't you?
she asks.
I don't.
I wear old brown
wool slippers.
With orthotics.
I try to imagine myself
strutting into the kitchen
before the kids
go to school,
making smoothies
and scrambled eggs
in my yoga pants,
my long gray sweatshirt,
and my four-inch
Lucite stilettos.
Click, click, click
go the heels
as I teeter toward
the tea cups.
Click, click, click
as I parade
with paper towels
to the place
where the cat
has retched.
Oh, Dolly,
as I slip into

these high-heeled thoughts
I thank you for dressing up the day.
These glammed up ideas
two-step and sashay
through the morning chores,
meanwhile my slippered self
marvels at the fun,
but shrugs—
I'm just so darn grateful
for arch support,
for the rubber soles
that ground me
as I sweep up the crumbs,
as I wipe the counters clean.
Grateful that when
the high-heeled thoughts
start to sing—
working nine to five—
they invite me
to sing along.

A Different Holding Pattern

If I am to hold the world in my heart,
then let me hold it the way leaves hold sunshine,
trapping the energy not for the sake of holding it,
but to transform it into nourishment.

Though the process isn't simple, it's common.
All around the globe, in every season,
leaves hold and synthesize
whatever the day gives them.

On a day when the energy of the world
seems too much to hold,
let me bid my heart turn
like a leaf to the sun and make sugar.

The way Rilke turned grief into sonnets.
The way Sibelius turned war into song.

FINDING MY CALLING

with a line from "After the Japanese" by Jack Granath

A warm March day
and the blue sky
slips itself
into the list
of things to do,
and I would have to be
deaf or just plain stubborn
not to hear the call
to play outside—
and damn, but
I'm stubborn,
so the world
sends a bobcat,
a red-tailed hawk
and a whole herd of elk
to the yard.
What's a busy woman
to do
but surrender?
I don't.
Head down, I get
the work done.
I put on the blinders
of responsibility
until a poem says to me,
You do the right thing,
citizen, and my chest pounds
in urgent code:
That. Means. You.
And I put down
the work and walk

into the day
to do my duty,
which is to meet the world
that will never
send an email,
the world
that will never knock,
will never call,
but will always
say welcome,
citizen, welcome.

FOR WHEN PEOPLE ASK

I want a word that means
  okay and *not okay,*
    more than that: a word that means
devastated and *stunned with joy.*
  I want the word that says
    I feel it all, all at once.
The heart is not like a songbird
  singing only one note at a time,
    more like a Tuvan throat singer
able to sing both a drone
  and simultaneously
    two or three harmonics high above it—
a sound, the Tuvans say,
  that gives the impression
    of wind swirling among rocks.
The heart understands swirl,
  how the churning of opposite feelings
    weaves through us like an insistent breeze,
leads us wordlessly deeper into ourselves,
  blesses us with paradox
    so we might walk more openly
into this world so rife with devastation,
  this world so ripe with joy.

LATENT

Riding our bikes through the warm summer night,
the dark itself parted to let us pass;
wind in our hair, soft whir of the wheels—
and an almost irrational joy grew in me then,
such simple joy, as if joy were always here,
waiting to flourish, needing only to be noticed.

And is joy latent in everything?
I have felt it sometimes in the washing
of dishes, in mowing the lawn,
in peeling the carrots, even washing
the fish tank and scrubbing the floor.

So could it be, too, inside worried pacing?
In envy? In sighing? In the clenching of fists?
Is there joy where I can't imagine it?
Joy—waiting to spin like a wheel,
waiting to rise like laughter
that careens through the deepening dark.

All Is Water

One river gives
its journey to the next.
  —Alberto Ríos, "When Giving Is All We Have"

I thought it was I giving the journey to you.
You gave your journey to me.

I thought I was the head waters,
but I have become your tributary.

Now I carry your turbulence. I carry your calm.
I carry the waters of my own breaking.

A river follows the same changing course,
but the water moving through is always new.

Let's name this river the river of sorrows.
Let's name it the river of love.

New, is it any wonder I am startled by this journey?
Old, is it any wonder I'm still longing to give?

Traveling these shores, there are moments
when I feel every other wave that has ever passed and

feel every wave that will ever be, and know
myself a share of something greater, something

generous that is always giving, something
ever borrowing from the current of the world.

AFTER THE TORTOISE WON THE RACE

It was the strangest thing.
She'd never cared before about winning.
Life had been about basking in the sun
at the entrance to her burrow.
Sometimes when she was warm enough,
she'd plod off in search of leaves.

Now, she thought about finish lines.
The feel of the ribbon on her prehistoric nose.
The roar of the crowd as she crossed.
They say tortoises don't have feelings,
no hippocampus in their small brains,
but she'd felt it, the tug of success.

She spent decades looking for another race
she had a chance to win. None of her friends
could understand. *Come dig in the sandy soil,*
they said, but it wasn't enough anymore.
She wished she'd never said yes to that race.
She wished she could race the hare again tonight.

She wished she could stop defining her life
by that one moment. Wished she could stop wishing
for any life beyond the life she had now,
sleeping in her burrow, cool and moist.
Wished all she wanted were soft weeds and long-leaf pines.
Wished she could hear that crowd. Just one more time.

May Morning

Just after sunrise,
I hear it, the bright airy trill
of the red-winged blackbird—
and before my eyes
are even open,
I feel a wild resonance
with the waking world,
the certainty I belong
to this day with its rising sun
and scent of green grass,
its breeze reaching in
through the screens;
I belong to this day
with my creature heart
that already this morning
longs to hold what it cannot,
longs to comfort others,
even knowing how
sorrow must be felt.
I belong to the song
of the red-winged blackbird
as it calls out again,
belong to the silence
as he waits for an answer.
And waits. And waits.
I belong to the spring
every bit as much
as I belong to winter.
This is perhaps
the conundrum of love,
no matter how strong the ache,
we still belong
to the world of beauty,

this world that calls to us
even in our sleep,
wakes us with a promise
strung like audible garland
across the dawn—
You belong, you belong.

INSTRUCTIONS FOR PERSEVERANCE

> Think less: Trust your inner animal.
> —Holiday Mathis, "Horoscopes by
> Holiday, December 19, 2020"

It's the chickadee
that saves me today.
Though the world
gets cold, the chickadee
stays. Despite snow.
Despite frost. Despite
lack of sun,
it doesn't leave
the winter land.
Oh, tough little bird
who sticks around,
who thrives
in any weather—
whose cheerful tune
spirals like hope
through the frigid
folds of December
as if to say, Let it come.
I can sing through
anything.
Let it come.

MONDAY NIGHT: A PORTRAIT

> You are not a passive observer in the cosmos. The entire
> universe is expressing itself through you at this very minute.
> —Deepak Chopra, *The Ultimate Happiness*
> *Prescription: 7 Keys to Joy and Enlightenment*

Even as she made the cauliflower soup,
she was a deep space explorer.
No one else in the room seemed to notice

she was floating. No one noticed
how gravity had no hold on her.
No, they only saw she was chopping onions,

noticed how the act made her cry. How was it
they did not hear her laughter, astonished
as she was by her own weightlessness,

by the way she could move in any direction?
Perhaps the novelty explains why
she forgot to turn off the stove,

untethered as she was to anything.
It's a miracle she sat at the dinner table at all,
what with the awareness that she was surrounded

by planets, spiral galaxies, black holes, moons. Yes,
miracle, she thought as she tasted the soup,
and noticed deep space not just around,

but inside her: supernovae, constellations,
interstellar dust,
the glorious, immeasurable dark.

AND MEAN IT, TOO

In every second, one hundred trillion neutrinos
pass through the body. One hundred trillion

subatomic particles move through us
as if we were sieves, no, as if we were nets

with holes so big that whole islands
travel through without our noticing.

It thrills me to think of the self so leaky.
Imagine if thoughts, too,

could clear us with so little friction,
so little effect. How many hopes and hurts

just today have I let stick? Imagine
them breezing through the aorta, imagine

them gliding through the brain, slipping through
the core of us, finding nowhere to anchor.

Imagine the miracle that in any given moment
we don't fall through our chair, our bed, the floor.

Imagine, permeable as we are, we still coalesce
enough to look at another, to see each other as whole.

We still manage to pick up a phone,
succeed in moving our holey lips,

and hundreds of trillions of neutrinos later,
with total certainty, manage to promise a solid I love you.

Imagine, with these pervious hands
we might carry each other,

might cradle each other,
might welcome each other home.

Meeting Some Truths

The truth was an avalanche—
an avalanche midsummer,
which is to say
it didn't seem possible,
but it happened.
And I was buried
beneath the cold
immense weight of it.
Crushed but still breathing—
another impossible truth.
I know some would like to see
the uprooted world
already green and lush again,
but anyone who
has wandered through
old avalanche paths
knows it takes many seasons
before the fallen old-growth trees
have moldered into soil,
many seasons before the new saplings
have grown into forest again.
The healing begins quickly,
but takes a long time.
Even then, the forest is never the same.
So much of transformation
happens beneath perception.
We all live in the avalanche path.

THERE IS ONLY THE FIELD

On the day my father begins hospice,
I watch the pronghorn in the field,
marvel as their brown and white-striped bodies
nearly disappear in the dead grass where
they graze. If only I could camouflage
my father so death can't find him, so that pain
would never have discovered him.
Tomorrow, my mother and brother and I
will gather around him the way a herd
might gather, circling him as some antelope
circle their young. But death will come.
And we, unable to run fast enough,
unable to hide, will meet it together.
And if I could fight death, would I?

Whatever horns I have
are more for ritual than attack.
When death arrives, I want to bring
my softest self. I won't bargain,
but I'll tell death it's taking the best of us—
the one who worked hardest to survive.
When death arrives, I want to ask it, *Please,
be gentle. He suffered so much already.*
I want to tell death, *You don't get all of him.*
I carry in me his goodness, his courage.
While I live, he will always be alive in this field.

III. Toward a Generous Elusive Grace

throwing my insecurity
into the bullring,
dressing it in red

ℬ

from beauty to beauty
devouring the crumb trail—
no going back

ℬ

this loving you—
both the net
and the high wire act

When the Audio Engineer Told Me She
Needed a Few Tracks of Me Laughing

I sat in the closet with a microphone and laughed,
spinning golden mirth out of nothing. I giggled
and chuckled and let the laugh grow
like a peony in spring, like the shimmer of a gong
when struck soft and often, like the scent of coffee
that starts in the kitchen but soon infuses every room.
The laugh began stilted, perhaps, but soon I was laughing
with honest glee like a baby amused by its own hand,
laughing like a woman who has lost something precious
and now knows the value of laughing. Laughing like
a weed seed that lands in an irrigated field. Laughing
like dry kindling found by a match. Laughing
like a puddle that expands in a downpour,
like a door that's picked its own latch. And the laughter
made so much space inside me—as if my inner map
had new boundaries drawn. As if I were released
from some old metal trap. And long after I'd recorded
a long track of laughter, I laughed. Till I cried, I laughed.

HELLO, FEAR

There I was, making tea in my kitchen,
when fear hit me like a school bus.
I didn't need a scientist or therapist
to tell me it hurt.
I screamed: *Arghh!* I shouted: *No!*

But after smashing into me,
fear just opened the folding glass door
of the bus, yanked me on,
then plopped me into a green vinyl seat.

I'm scared, I said.
Yeah, fear said. *'Cause I'm scary.*

Yeah, I squealed, as the bus careened
through the couch, through
my bedroom, through the splintering
dining room table.

What if I lose everything? I said to fear.
Yeah, said fear, *what if you do?*

And who will I be when everything changes?
Yeah, said fear, *who will you be?*

Then fear opened the door
and shoved me off the bus
and I was standing again beside
the familiar green counter,
tea cup in hand, not a drop spilled.

Who will you be? fear shouted
from the half-open window.

I took a deep breath,
not knowing how to respond,
then stepped into my life,
determined to live into the answer.

Lesson from the Water Ouzel

Sometimes I want to be anywhere but here,
but today, I let myself feel it all.

I go to the river covered in ice
and move along the bank until

I find the open places where the dark-feathered ouzel
chooses to submerge in the cold, cold water—

It doesn't hesitate to plunge into frigid depths.
It knows it was made for this.

Coming Together

Driving over Dallas Divide
I thought how not all streams
are destined to come together—
at least not for a long, long time.
Imagine, two snowflakes landed
side by side atop the Divide. Come spring,
one might flow west to the San Miguel,
the other east to the Uncompahgre.
It would be over a hundred miles
of flowing through beaver dams
and irrigation ditches, rapids
and eddies, before the waters
could meet again.
And so it is tonight, I feel a rush
of gratefulness that however
it happened, you and I have somehow
managed to be moving right now through
these landscapes of change together.
Think of all of the paths
that could have pulled us apart.
And yet here we are, you and I,
moving across and around obstacles,
you and I traveling together
through everything the world
has thrown at us, you and I,
diverging and coming back together,
two bodies, many possible paths,
one water.

GROUNDHOG DAY

May I not only see my own shadow,
but may I let it wrestle me
the way an angel once met Jacob
then wrestled him till dawn.
May we scrabble and scrap
until I am trembling, exhausted,
until the shadow dislocates what I think I know
about how to move through the world,
until panting, I beg it to bless me,
cling to it until it gives me a new name.
I want to know everything
I am capable of—the destruction,
the ferocity, the benediction.
I don't need to know the weather.
I just want to know I can meet
whatever comes, even
the darkest parts of myself,
and learn from them,
then limp into the daylight
toward healing, toward wholeness.

TRUST

It's the wing inside the empty room,
the wing inside the shiver,
the sprightly wing inside the ash,
the wing inside the lover.
The wing inside of silence
before the impossible words,
the wing that flutters moonlessly,
the wing inside the shards.
And a thousand thousand tiny wings
flutter inside each breath—
and I forget the wings are here,
until I meet an edge—

BEYOND TOUCH

And if a cheek should find a chest,
and if a tongue should graze a lip,
and if a hand should meet a curve,
and if a hip should stir a hip,
then we might know the flesh as kindling,
know the skin as eager spark,
know the lover as the flame
that helps unthaw the frozen dark.
But if a heart should stoke a heart,
and if a soul should fuel a soul,
then we might know the self as unself—
ravaged, ardent, blazing, whole.

WHEN LIVING ON A TINY ISLAND

It was a dream, but I tell you
everything was on fire in the house—
I knew the whole island would burn,
and I had to choose what to take
and I ran past the old records
and thought, I have those songs in me,
and I ran past the books
and thought, I have those stories,
and I ran past the photos
and thought, those memories
are already with me,
so I ran, chased by flames,
toward the ocean
with the only thing
I could really carry, this buoyant love,
and I dove in. My hands, empty,
could cup the water
and pull through the tide.
The salt water lifted me,
whispered in waves: *Letting go*
is what keeps you alive.

PRACTICING KONMARI

I did it. Exactly as Marie Kondo said:
I removed everything
from my closets and drawers,
and touched each thing—
every sock, every shirt, every shoe—
and I asked each item, *Do you bring me joy?*

Joy, it turns out, likes many clothes.
Long scarves. Wide necklines.
Black pants. Long knit dresses
and tall leather boots.
Second-hand cashmere sweaters
and many gardening gloves.

And all the while I touched my clothes,
I did as Marie said,
I visualized the life I want,
which is apparently a life
in which my closet is full of black pants
and scarves and tall leather boots—
a life in which I talk to my clothes
and smile as they whisper back to me,
Joy, joy, joy.

PRACTICAL APPLICATION

Knowing now how one moment
rewrites every moment after it;
how in an instant, the heart can trip
over its own beat and need to be retaught
how to love; how irreversible takes
only a second to say and yet
contains all eternity; how quickly our breath
can be claimed by the tides of forever,

for this I buy deep pink tulips for the table.
For this I make Dutch apple pie.
For this I walk through the canyon
in moonlight. I remind myself: no guarantees.
For this, I pull you in and hold you. For this,
I stand still in the spruce trees and breathe.

AT LAST

After a week, at last the peaches
on the counter smell like peaches,
their sweet summer scent reaching
across the room to where I sit
trying to balance numbers.
The scent is like a flirty lover
who won't take no for an answer,
who trails fingertips down my cheek
and neck and lightly tugs at my collar,
then tilts my head back
to whisper into my ear,
*Isn't there something you'd rather
be doing, my dear?*
And damn if I'm not distracted
and hungry and all I want
is to sink my teeth into peach
and that's what I do.
So much of life feels like letting go,
but tonight life says,
Pick me up, sweetheart. Take me in.
And the gold sticky juice
runs all over those numbers.
I lick my fingers clean.

EMILY DICKINSON IN HOUSTON

And as I merge onto the interstate
with its ten lanes of traffic and
semis and tolls, Emily sits primly
in the back seat and doesn't
say a word. She was a bit reluctant
to come along—we're a long way
from Amherst, after all—but
she admitted she was tired
of the New England weather
and longed for something new.
As it is, it's raining in Houston,
and the puddles on the pavement
splash up onto the windshield
and I grip the wheel more tightly,
sensing Emily's rising panic.
All around us cars weave
and unweave, changing lanes,
charging the world with an unbraiding
rush. Then she says in a voice so quiet
I can barely hear it beneath
the hum of passing cars,
I loved someone once. It felt
something like this. Beside us,
a siren wails. *Yes,* she says,
fisting the white skirts of her dress,
Yes, it was exactly like this.

FIRST LOVE

Tonight, it comes back, how we'd go for walks
in the tall dry grass behind the old school.
In my memory, the field goes on and on and
it never rains and we have no idea how young
we are. Sun-drunk and heat-starved, twin ripples
of wind. Broken grass in our hair and howl
in our skin. And we believed in forever then—

perhaps we touched it those summer days,
a strand of forever, forgotten for decades,
lost amongst other eternal strands—but oh,
those hands, those parted lips, that tall, trembling grass.

The Key Speaks

I couldn't believe
she tossed me
into the back of the car—
after all, a key
is an important thing.
But toss me she did.

You should have seen
her face when she
shut the driver's door
and all the car doors locked,
me sitting there
on the back seat.

That can't happen,
she said. But it did.
That can't happen,
she repeated,
as if her words
might change the world.

But everyone knows
words won't open
a locked door.
She's still ranting,
walking circles
around the locked car.

How many innocent choices
have pitiless consequences?
Tossing a key. Not
washing your hands.
Not saying I love you
when given the chance.

In the Fourth of July Parade

Right down the middle of main street
the woman with the long red braids
and fairy wings strapped to her back
rode a unicycle more than two times
taller than she was—rode it with balance
and grace, her arms stretched out,
as if swimming through gravity,
as if embracing space—her smile an invitation
to join in her bliss. How simple it is, really,
to make of ourselves a gate that swings open
to the joy that is. How simple, like tossing
candy in a parade, to share the key to the gate.

Contact Joy

He cleans the base of the skis
with a fine, steel brush to remove
the old wax, his body swaying
above the ski, tip to tail, tip to tail,
so the micro hairs on the base
will lie down in the direction of travel
on snow. A fine copper brush
cleans it more. His movements
are quick, precise, a dance
that now comes naturally.
The only music is the sound
of the brushes, the sound
of his breath. There is no
laughter, no joking,
not even a smile, but
sometimes on winter nights
I walk toward the light
in the garage and watch
his body intent on its work,
and I feel the quiet joy
he finds in preparation
and the work of foundation,
and his joy seeps into me,
soft as the darkness
that holds the garage,
deep as the space
that holds us all.

EVOLUTION

We drove seven hours,
and half the time it snowed,
so I kept my eyes fixed
to the slushy road, but
there was the moment
when I looked at my girl
in the passenger seat
and fell in love in an instant
and stroked her hair
and she, catching my gaze,
offered me her open hand—

for this moment,
the first tetrapods evolved
in shallow and swampy freshwater,
for this moment,
the ichthyostega formed
arms and finger bones,
and though it took
thirty-million years
of primate and homo sapien change—
changes in facial muscles and
the cingulate cortex of the brain—
for this moment
we learned to smile.

SELF-PORTRAIT AS SUBORDINATE CLAUSE

and when
the larkspur
petals fall and when
the fall begins to sing
and when the song weaves
through the loss and when
the loss dyes
everything, when
everything is
emptier and emptiness
is whole somehow, when
whole is what a life
does, when life is
what is now, when
now is
ever changing
and changing knows
no end, when
any ending
I might seek is
just another
when

UNTAMED

We measure the afternoon in wild raspberries,
pulling to our mouths the abundant ripe fruits
like the feral beings we are.

Fingers stained red and lips stained red
and the moments stained red with joy.
If it is not smart to speak of love,

then let me not be smart.
Let me speak of love that flourishes
like wild raspberries in a rainy summer.

Let me live into love as undomesticated
as these brambles that line the creeks.
Let me remember today

by the sweet and tart taste of wild berries,
how softly they fell into our palms.
Let me be as eager for love

as the look on my daughter's face
when she dragged me by the hand
back to the raspberry patch, saying, *More, more.*

BUSHWHACK

I followed the road as if it were a teacher.
It went up, I went up. It turned, I turned.
It was a long time before I relearned
the road is not the only way to go.
The first day I walked away from the gravel,
I fell. That was the day I learned
staying upright is not what's most important.

Traveling the Same Road

You *idiot*, is what you say
to the driver five cars ahead of you
on the two-lane road that winds
through the river canyon.
There is no passing lane,
and you feel the crush
of the minutes as they rub against each other
while the white SUV five cars ahead
does not pull over
in the wide spot on the road
where all conscientious slow drivers know
to pull over to let the other drivers pass.
Idiot, you grumble, and miss
any beauty outside the window—
red rock cliffs and diamonding streams—
focused as you are on the speedometer,
the brake. Once it was you,
a girl of fifteen, who drove so cautiously
the winding roads to church
on a Sunday morning, that first day
with your driver's permit.
And who was it in the long line
behind you who called the police
to report a drunk driver?
When the police pulled you over,
not one but two squad cars
with blaring red and blue lights,
you didn't cry when the officers laughed—
there was warmth in their relief
to find that you were not drunk, but young.
No, you cried after they walked away,
cried all the way to mass.
Bless them, the irate ones,

the ones who fume in the back,
the ones who think furious thoughts.
That's right. Bless yourself,
you, the livid one who even now
is hurling names at the other travelers
on the same paved path.
Settle in. Sixteen miles under the speed limit
will give you time to think about
how we're all traveling
the same winding road
no matter which route we take—
all of us pilgrims journeying toward
a generous, elusive grace.

One Thing to Do with a Fist

wrap it around
a bouquet of gold and orange calendula,
now offer it to someone else—
how easily their smile
opens your hand

BALD EAGLE

In less than ten seconds
I fell in love with the eagle
before it rounded the corner
and disappeared.

Sometimes,
it's easier to love
that which moves quickly
through our lives.

Harder to love
what stays long enough
to disappoint, to hurt, to betray—
harder to feel disenchanted
and love anyway.

I've seen an eagle
carry prey that weighs
more than it does.

Makes me want to believe
I, too, can carry more—
like a love bigger than I am.
Like forgiveness beyond
what my thoughts can think.
Like willingness to keep loving
long after I'd rather rest my wings.

IV. Unfolding into the Moment

unable to find a door to escape
I close my eyes and find
I am the door

&

     all day I spike my tea with sky—
      is it any wonder by night
       I'm singing love songs

&

heaven
earth
this day a ladder

BECOMING

The hurt you embrace becomes joy.
—Jalāl ad-Dīn Muhammad Rūmī
translated by Coleman Barks, "Silkworms"

To wake and not want
to change anything.
To let the heart feel
what it feels.
To be disarmed,
defenseless
and so alive.
There are days
love claims us
so utterly
we unfold
into the moment,
whatever it holds,
certain we were made for it.
Nothing has prepared us
for this.
Everything
has prepared us
for this.

ON A DAY WHEN THE WORLD
HAS ITS WAY WITH ME

Like every day, this day
it is clear that only love
will save us. Not in the grandiose

abstract way, but in the alarmingly
specific way. As in forgiveness, now.
As in choosing to hold our own hand instead

of swinging back. As in taking
three deep breaths before saying
something we regret. Love saves us

from thirsting in the desert of our lives,
but only if we save it first by
choosing it, now in this moment

of angry words, now in this moment
of clenched thoughts, now in
this moment when we'd rather

taste venom, but instead, we
pour love into our cup and
bring it to our lips and drink and drink

and offer it to others, until once again
only love makes sense,
only love refills the cup.

Making It Right: A Prophecy

> The duty of a musician is for us to take anything that
> happens on stage and make it part of the music.
> —Herbie Hancock, MasterClass

No wrong notes in jazz, said the musician
and the poet insisted, no wrong words.
No wrong leaf, said the tree,
and field said, no wrong grass.
No wrong time, promised the friend,
and the river said, no wrong rock.
And the heart said, no wrong love,
but the mind said, no, that's wrong.
And the wrong love replanted itself like grass
and grew wild in all the wrong places
like a gorgeous weed, like a tap-rooted song
until the whole field was beautifully wrong, wrong.

UNITY

Today we lose the words
yours and mine and find
in their absence a song
that can only be sung together.
How did we ever think
we could attempt
this humanness alone?
To the table of love,
we bring soup, bring cherries,
bring the bread of our own
sweet communion.
We bring scissors to cut away
the tresses of the past,
bring dark wine to toast
the courage of showing up exposed.
And when we forget
the words to the song,
well, there is always laughter.
And when we forget to laugh,
well, there is always
the union of tears—
the way many rivers
become one river,
the way many voices
become one music.

SURRENDER

Some mornings I wake and the peace
I tried to find yesterday finds me—
arrives in the open palms of the river scent,
in the erratic path of the warbler,
in the low golden angle of sun as it slants
through the gray-knuckled branches of cottonwood trees.
Even the broken watering can seems to bring me
news of what's been here all along—
the peace that holds up the turmoil, the mess.
And the dried grasses in the field
and the tiny new leaves on the currants
gather me into them. They're like old friends who say,
*It's okay, make all the mistakes you want
around us.* Some mornings, through no effort
of our own, we are gathered into the peace
of the patient lichen and the still pond.
It's the difference between breathing
and being breathed, between asking for grace
and finding that grace has been asking for us.

FOR THE LIVING

with a line paraphrased from Wendy Videlock

It is the work of the living
to grieve the dead.
It is our work to wake each day,
to live into the world that is.
It is our work to weep,
and it is our work to be healed.
Some part of us knows
not only the absence of our beloveds,
but also their presence,
how they continue to teach us,
how they invite us to grow.
It is our work to be softened by loss,
to be undone, destroyed, remade.
Wounded, we recoil,
and it is our work to notice how,
like crushed and trampled grass,
we spring back.
It is our work to meet death again
and again and again,
and though it aches to be open,
it is our work to be opened,
to live into the opening
until we know ourselves
as blossoms nourished from within
by the radiance of the ones
who are no longer physically here.
They have given us their love light to carry.
It is our work to be in service to that light.

ANTI-LAMENT

There was that summer
    when my record player broke,
        the needle always returning

to the first song and playing
    the whole record again and again,
        through morning, through midnight,

and so George Winston's *Winter into Spring*
    played all through my summer.
        Soft and pensive, each melodic phrase

hung spare in the air as if inviting
    revelation or breath
        before burbling forward like snowmelt.

How I loved that summer,
    every moment of it kissed
        with chords shattered into arpeggios,

silences and grace notes.
    Sometimes breaking brings a gift
        we didn't know we needed,

the way a broken record player
    steeped me for months
        in the grace of a melancholic loveliness

and made the haunting familiar.
    The way a broken heart can bring up
        a record of beautiful memories,

one after another, day after day,
        and somehow heal us by making of the wreckage
            a masterpiece.

The Softening

I carry it with me now, everywhere I go,
this softness, this limp unstuffed toy, a puppy
with a thin square body made for snuggling.

I carry it in my purse where it mingles
with my wallet, my glasses, my lipstick,
my loss. When I'm walking, I reach in
and let my fingers rub its soft, worn fleece.

When I'm watching a movie, once it's dark,
I pull it out and let Skinny Puppy settle in my lap,
as if its brown embroidered eyes could see.
I know it's just an object, but it's a well-loved object,
some small proof that my boy was here,
that he loved, loved hard, loved long.

I remember how he carried Skinny to school,
clutching the small brown scrap to his belly
when we would say goodbye. I remember how,
long after the toy trains and model tractors
and even the complicated Legos had gone away,
Skinny still slept on his pillow.

It's been worn down by love, this old friend,
and made even softer by the loving—
like me, an older woman who has become
frayed, sentimental, slightly tattered,
distressed, but so shaped by love, and softened,
yes, softened. Even more myself, only softer.

IN THE GARDEN, AGAIN

After breaking, after kneeling,
after raising my ripe fist,
after opening my palm, after
clenching it again, after running,
after hiding, after taking off
my masks, after stilling,
after shouting, after bargaining
with God, after crumpling
and cursing, after losing,
after song, after seeking,
after breath, after breath,
after breath,
I stand in the sunflowers
of early September
and watch as the bees weave
from one giant bloom to another,
and I, too, am sunflower,
tall-stemmed and face lifted,
shaped by the love of light
and the need for rain.
I stand here until some part of me
is again more woman than sunflower,
and she notices how,
for a few moments,
it was enough just to be alive.
Just to be alive, it was enough.

Sunday Morning

A soft-poached egg
and a slice of pumpernickel toast,
a cup of English Breakfast
and a chair at a round table in a sunlit room
beside an old friend, laughing and talking—
there are moments so ordinary
as to be perfect—moments
we feel so completely ourselves
we don't try to hold on to the minutes.
Such moments don't try
to put themselves in a picture frame,
don't pretend to be necessary or grand.
They ask us for nothing except
that we spend them like change,
as if we had a lifetime supply.

ENDINGS FOR BEGINNERS

With a punch line, of course.
Or an invitation.
With a twist. Or a kiss.
Or an unanswerable question.
By circling back to the beginning.
Or with a bang. Or a whimper.
With a call to action.
With a five-course dinner.
With a clincher,
or a cliffhanger,
but not with a preposition.
Endings feel best
when of your own volition.
End with a flourish
or a touch of cream.
On a high note. With a strong quote.
By making a scene.
End with a period.
Or end with a handshake.
End with an exclamation point.
Or end with heartbreak.
It's okay to tie
or to end in a draw,
but don't end with ellipses
that just make things go on ...
and on ...
and on ... .
End in a fiasco.
Or end with a song.
End with a reversal.
End with a bell.
End with a cry
that All is well.

End with purpose
or allegory.
Every bit of our lives
is made of stories,
stories that end
so new stories begin,
so end well, end well.
Then start again.

BEGINNING

Grief arrives with an eraser—
  not the cute pink kind
   at the end of a pencil,
more like the big gray kind
  with the fat felt strips
   we used on chalk boards—
the kind that didn't really
  get rid of what was there,
   just smeared it around
until it was unrecognizable,
  the ghost of what was written
  still haunting the board.
At first I thought
  what was being erased
  was the one who was gone.
Then I realized
  what's being erased is me—
  whatever I think I know
about love, about life,
  about death.
  This erasure is nothing
I would have asked for.
  But now, lines blurring,
  what is infinite in me begins
to recognize itself,
  and it's beautiful—
  this spaciousness
I once thought
  meant the end.

At Five

Along the lake and down the hill,
the road dead-ended into a meadow
with a wooden fence a girl could slip through,

and slip through she did,
that five-year-old version of me,
she slipped through the gaps into tall green grass

and then wandered to the lake
where the weeping willow hung over the shoreline
and she could sit beneath its shade and disappear—

or perhaps more rightly, she could show up.
As herself. Show up not as a girl who lived up the road
but as shade, as shore, as tree,

as field, as green beyond the fence.
Perhaps it only happened once or twice,
that journey past the dead end,

but forty-seven years later, I remember
the dissolution, how beneath that tree
I was no longer who I was, only more so.

I knew myself as integral to the miracle.
There were whole decades I forgot her,
that infinite version of me.

Tonight I can tell she never left.
How did she ever fit in my limited sense of self?
What does she have to teach me now

of fences, of shadows,
of sitting quietly,
of the art of slipping through?

POROSITY

And so I learn I am porous—
learn I am not just dust,
but soil. Everything
moves through me.
I am not the container
I believed myself to be,
but a portion of earth
more other than self.

In a dream, I was told,
The body is permeable
to life and to death.

I want to remember
that voice. I want to remember
how it feels to be earth,
to know the self as both living
and dead.

I want to remember how absence
has never felt more holy,
how its sacredness is rivaled
only by the holiness of what's here.

No separation, said the voice.
Remember.

I want to remember
the infinite dark inside
each infinite moment,
how both soil and time
are planted with stars.

Oh, sweet teachings
I cannot understand,
how they spiral out
like galaxies inside me,
how they slip
like loose soil through my hands.

FORTUNATE

Tonight, I want to break into the fortune cookie factory
armed with millions of tiny rectangular papers
I'd surreptitiously slip into the thin folded wafers.
You will say five nice things in the next hour, says one.
Another: *You'll bake something nice for your neighbor.*
Every fortune will predict a generosity of spirit:
A grudge you've been gripping will disappear,
or *Gratitude for the smallest things will flood you.*
And on the back, it will acknowledge that to make
any number lucky, you'll simply write a check
using that number to a local charity—
the more zeroes you add to the number,
the luckier that number will be.
Perhaps a better idea:
Fill each cookie with a blank slip of paper—
some small scrap of potential that invites every person
to write their own fortune, invites them to feel
like the author of their own destiny. In fact, here.
Here's a pen. And a very small white page.
You don't even need the cookie.

I Want an Interlude with Mr. Clean

want to find him in my kitchen
with his big muscled arms
and his spotless white shirt.

Call me James, he'll say, as I
pour him a glass of sauvignon blanc.
He'll pull out a permanent marker

and write his name on the glass.
What are you doing? I'll gasp.
When I'm around, there's a world

of crafty possibilities, he'll say.
Then he'll whip out his trusty white magic eraser
and swipe the permanent marker away.

Then he'll give me a spin—
Open for me your oven door.
Oh James, I'll say, *you don't mean ...*

... that I will bring my legendary clean
to your oven glass? Why yes, Rosemerry,
I can lift away grease buildup from hard-to-clean places.

He'll give me a flex. *Kitchen sink next?*
He'll swagger across the room.
I'll swoon. *James, I never knew you'd be so, so ...*

... adept at sticky residue? he'll suggest,
and I'll guide his hand to my
faucet. *Say goodbye to water spots,*

he'll say with a grin, his teeth glistening
like brand-new white backsplash tile,
like unused linoleum,

and we'll dance together
across the sparkling floor, sponges in hand,
drawn to whatever is dirty.

And the room will smell of meadows
and bleach and rain. *And oh darling*, he'll say,
don't you think it's time you took me to the bath?

SIMPLE TOOLS

I am so grateful for the rubber spatula,
the way it sits quietly in the drawer
yet is always ready for action—
is game to scrape the walls of the blender
or to fold chocolate chips into dough.
It evens and swirls the frosting on cake
and welcomes the tongue
of a child. In a sharp world,
it knows the value of being blunt;
it knows that to smooth is a gift to the world.
Some people are knives, and
I thank them. Me, I want to belong
to the order of spatulas—those
who blend, who mix, who co-mingle
dissimilars to create a cohesive whole.
I want to spread sweetness, to be a workhorse
for beauty, to stir things up,
to clean things out. I want to be useful,
an instrument of unity, a means, a lever for life.

BELONGING

And if it's true we are alone,
we are alone together,
the way blades of grass
are alone, but exist as a field.
Sometimes I feel it,
the green fuse that ignites us,
the wild thrum that unites us,
an inner hum that reminds us
of our shared humanity.
Just as thirty-five trillion
red blood cells join in one body
to become one blood.
Just as one hundred thirty-six thousand
notes make up one symphony.
Alone as we are, our small voices
weave into the one big conversation.
Our actions are essential
to the one infinite story
of what it is to be alive.
When we feel alone,
we belong to the grand communion
of those who sometimes feel alone—
we are the dust, the dust that hopes,
a rising of dust, a thrill of dust,
the dust that dances in the light
with all other dust, the dust
that makes the world.

TWO TRUTHS

after Ruth Stone, "Train Ride"

He is dead. Never again
to pull on the fencing mask,
moonwalk to his bedroom
or snuggle on the couch.
Not dancing on the stage.
He is dead. Not spinning
the gator through the field.
Not graphing equations for pleasure.
Is he dead? asks the heart.
No, he lives on forever.
In the scent of lemon.
In the cloudy ice on the pond.
In the buds of the lilac tree.
In the song on my breath. He lives
in blue sky and comet and field.
He lives in ink and in spaces between.
He is dead.
I held his unbreathing body in my arms.
Since that day, he has never left me.
He is alive forever.

No Regret

Some moments are flame.
There was a time
I wanted a promise
we would not burn.
Now I give myself to the blaze
knowing the burn
is part of the path,
knowing that matter
dances best
once it's ash.

WHAT'S IN A BROKEN CUP?

Not everything broken
need be fixed.
Even the loveliest cup,
the one that seemed perfection,
the one that fit
just right in the hand
and held the favorite wine,
even that cup is only a cup,
and, being fashioned
out of breakable clay,
it was, we could say,
made to be broken.
The fact it was fragile
was always a part of its value.
In shattered fragments,
the cup is no less
treasured—perhaps
even more treasured now
that its wholeness
isn't taken for granted.
There are some who
would throw the pieces away.
There are some who
would meet them with
glue or even with gold
in an effort to repair.
But there are some
who will cherish what is broken,
hold it even more tenderly now,
trusting its use—
though different—
is no less valuable.
Trusting a fragment

is sometimes more than enough.
Trusting we might now
sip our wine
straight from the source.

A Bouquet of Long-Stemmed Gratefulnesses

Thank you to my husband Eric, my daughter Vivian and my step-daughter Shawnee and her husband Drew for their unending love and support.

Mom, thank you for everything, and I mean everything.

Thank you to Elizabeth Dilly and Steven Nightingale for their vision, their invitation, their passion, and their hard work.

Thank you to Joan Shapiro for her copy editing superpowers.

Thank you to Bob Blesse for his wisdom in how to shape a page and how to craft a cover, and also for his incredible patience.

Thank you to Joanie Schwarz for her ability to capture a moment in a frame.

And thank you to all the friends and companion poets who have carried me with your love and encouragement. A thousand thousand thank yous.

END NOTES

"Emerging Self-Portrait": It is said that Beethoven, when he was increasingly deaf, began to play the piano louder and louder. At one point, his friends complained he struck the keys too violently, and he mildly rebuked them, saying, *Ist es nicht schön?* (Is it not beautiful?)

"Revival": The epigraph is from a private conversation with Mirabai Starr.

"From What I've Tasted of Desire": The title is from "Fire and Ice" by Robert Frost, published in *New Hampshire* (Henry Holt, 1923).

"Seeking Purpose": The epigraph is from *He Can Who Thinks He Can, and Other Papers on Success in Life* by Orison Swett Marden (Ulan Press, 2012).

"With the Stars All Around": I wrote this poem about a week before my son died. I thought it was for him. A week later, I realized how much this poem was for me.

"The Question": I was at a dance recital in a packed auditorium when my beloved friend and mentor Jude Jordan Kalush told me the question she asks herself, "Is this the path of love?" It changed me from that moment on.

"Meeting Your Death": In Gregory Orr's poem "This is what was bequeathed us" in *How Beautiful the Beloved* (Copper Canyon Press, 2009), Orr writes "the beloved's clear instructions: Turn me into song; sing me awake." And I love these lines so much, but when I wrote this poem, I couldn't find any clear instructions. Perhaps I envied Orr his clarity, took my own muddledness as an invitation to lean deeper into the moment, to be more open, to listen more.

"More Love, More Love": The epigraph is from *Riding Shotgun* by Rita Mae Brown (Random House Publishing Group, 1997).

"Finding My Calling": "After the Japanese" by Jack Granath is printed in *Rattle* (Summer 2008).

"For When People Ask": I thank my friend Mariah Blackhorse for offering these two suggestions for the word I want. From Japanese, *setsunai*, "the ability to carry sorrow and joy at once" and from Greek, charmolypi, "sweet joy-making sorrow." These words are part of the *Positive Lexicography* curated by Tim Lomas, PhD. Also, in strange and beautiful news, the morning we buried my son in the Telluride cemetery, as we began to pull the dirt into the grave, we heard, loud and clear from the town park stage about a half a mile away, a Tuvan throat singer begin to sing. It resonated through our box canyon, and it was everything this poem describes and more.

"All Is Water": The epigraph is from "When Giving Is All We Have" by Alberto Ríos in *A Small Story about the Sky* (Copper Canyon Press, 2015). The title is a quote from Thaleus of Miletus.

"Instructions for Perseverance": The epigraph is by the amazing astrologer Holiday Mathis. If your newspaper doesn't carry "Horoscopes by Holiday," you can tell the editor that they should. You can also find her horoscopes online at www.holidaymathis.com.

"Monday Night: A Portrait": The epigraph is from *The Ultimate Happiness Prescription: 7 Keys to Joy and Enlightenment* by Deepak Chopra (Harmony, 2009).

"Coming Together": You can trace a raindrop anywhere in the country to see where it ends up. https://river-runner.samlearner.com/

"Groundhog Day": This poem refers to the story in *Genesis* 32:22-32.

"Practicing KonMari": This poem refers to the book *The Life-Changing Magic of Tidying Up: The Japanese Art of Decluttering and Organizing* by Marie Kondo (Ten Speed Press, 2014).

"Becoming": The epigraph is from "Silkworms," a translation of Jalāl ad-Dīn Muhammad Rūmī, by Coleman Barks, and it can be found in *The Glance: Songs of Soul-Meeting* (Penguin Compass, 1999).

"Making It Right: A Prophesy": The epigraph is a quote from Herbie Hancock's MasterClass, available at www.masterclass.com.

"Surrender": The quote in the poem, attributed to "old friends," was actually said to me by beloved friend and author Craig Childs—because, of course, I had just made a mistake. His generous response stays with me.

"For the Living": The night my son died, I was walking in the dark on a road in Georgia, talking with my dear friend Wendy Videlock. She said to me, "He has given you his love light to carry." At that very moment, a firefly lit up about six inches in front of my face. Her words felt like a charge, an invitation for how to meet the unmeetable, and they framed every moment that has come since then with a lens of love and legacy.

"Anti-Lament": This poem was in part inspired by "Anti-Lamentation," a poem I love by Dorianne Laux found in *The Book of Men* (W.W. Norton & Company, 2011). I love the invitation to write an anti-lament, to "Regret nothing," as she says.

"I Want an Interlude with Mr. Clean": This poem is inspired by "I'm in Love with the Morton Salt Girl" by Richard Peabody from *I'm in Love with the Morton Salt Girl* (Paycock Press, 1985). It is so much fun to write a poem about falling in love with a mascot or product character—try it! Apparently, Mr. Clean's real name is Veritably, which came from a "Give Mr. Clean a First Name" promotion in 1962.

"Simple Tools": This poem was written as a challenge. One night my beloved friend Christie Aschwanden told me, "You cannot write a poem about a rubber spatula." Ahem. It is in conversation with "Sifter" by Naomi Shihab Nye found in *A Maze Me: Poems for Girls* (Greenwillow Books, 2005), in which she writes about how her English teacher gave the assignment to write about how you are like a kitchen implement. I recommend it.

"Two Truths": This poem was inspired by "Train Ride" by Ruth Stone, found in *Send My Roots Rain: A Companion on the Grief Journey* by Kim Langley (Paraclete Press, 2019).

Acknowledgments

Thank you to the following publications that first published poems found in *All the Honey*, sometimes in previous versions.

A First Sip: "Filling My Purse with Commas," "From What I've Tasted of Desire," "On a Day When the World Has Its Way with Me"

American Life in Poetry: "In the Fourth of July Parade"

Braided Way: "And Mean It, Too," "Monday Night: A Portrait," "Simple Tools," "There Is Only the Field," "Watching My Friend Pretend Her Heart Isn't Breaking"

Bristlecone: "Trust"

Clover: "I Want an Interlude with Mr. Clean," "Losing It," "One Thing to Do with a Fist," "Traveling the Same Road"

For the Brokenhearted (Napping Dog Press): "Becoming"

Gratefulness.org: "Belonging," "Temple," "For When People Ask," "The Invitation," "May Morning"

How to Love the World: Poems of Gratitude and Hope, ed. James Crews (Storey Publishing): "Hope"

Imperfect II (History House Publishers): "Hello, Fear"

Limp Wrist: "Making Breakfast with Dolly"

ONE ART: "After the Tortoise Won the Race," "Allium," "Revival," "In the Garden, Again"

The Path to Kindness: Poems of Connection and Joy, ed. James Crews (Storey Publishing): "The Question"

Spiritual Directors International Journal: "Beginning"

Stone Gathering: "Practicing KonMari"

Twenty Bellows: "Finding My Calling"

ABOUT THE AUTHOR

Rosemerry Wahtola Trommer lives with her husband and daughter in Placerville, Colorado, on the banks of the wild and undammed San Miguel River. She served as San Miguel County's first poet laureate (2007-2011) and as Western Slope Poet Laureate (2015-2017).

Devoted to helping others explore their creative potential, Rosemerry is the co-host of Emerging Form, a podcast on creative process, co-founder of Secret Agents of Change (a surreptitious kindness cabal), and co-leader of Soul Writers Circle. She also directed the Telluride Writers Guild for ten years and co-hosted Telluride's Talking Gourds Poetry Club.

She teaches and performs poetry for mindfulness retreats, women's retreats, teachers, addiction recovery programs, scientists, hospice, literary burlesque and more. Clients include Camp Coca Cola, Craig Hospital, Business & Professional Women, Think 360, Ah Haa School, Desert Dharma, Well for the Journey, and the Women's Dermatological Society.

She believes in the power of practice and has been writing a poem a day since 2006. Her daily poems can be found at: https://ahundredfallingveils.com/.

She has been a satsang student of Joi Sharp since 2010.

She has 12 collections of poetry, and her work has appeared in O Magazine, A Prairie Home Companion, PBS News Hour, American Life in Poetry, on fences, in back alleys, on Carnegie Hall Stage and on hundreds of river rocks she leaves around town.

She's won the Fischer Prize, Rattle's Ekphrastic Challenge (thrice), the Dwell Press Solstice Prize, the Writer's Studio Literary Contest (twice) and The Blackberry Peach Prize.

She's been an organic fruit grower, a newspaper and magazine editor, and a parent educator for Parents as Teachers. She's now writing a novel. She earned her MA in English Language & Linguistics at UW-Madison. Her website can be found at: www.wordwoman.com.

One-word mantra: Adjust.
Three-word mantra: I'm still learning.

Colophon

The text typeface is Quadraat, designed by Dutch type designer, Fred Smeijers, and first commercially released in 1992. Quadraat combines Renaissance elegance with contemporary ideas on construction and form. The calligraphic typeface on the cover is Rialto, designed by Austrian Lui Karner and Italian Giovanni de Faccio in 1995. It is named for the famous bridge in Venice, Italy.

Designed and produced by Robert Blesse.

Printed and bound by McNaughton & Gunn, Saline, Michigan.

This is the second publication of Samara Press.